JIM BRIDGER

Frontiersman and Mountain Guide

CHARLES W. MAYNARD

The Rosen Publishing Group's

PowerKids Press™

New York

For Anna, a hiker and explorer extraordinaire

"I defy the annals of chivalry to furnish the record of a life more wild and perilous than that of a Rocky Mountain trapper."—Francis Parkman, an American historian who traveled on the Oregon Trail to Fort Laramie in 1846

Published in 2003 by The Rosen Publishing Group, Inc.
29 East 21st Street, New York, NY 10010

First Edition

Managing Editor: Kathy Kuhtz Campbell
Book Designer: Maria E. Melendez

Photo Credits: Cover and title page, James Bridger, date unknown © Kansas State Historical Society; p. 4 (top) © Daguerreotype Collection, Library of Congress Prints and Photographs Division; pp. 4 (bottom), 7 (top and bottom), 10 © Nancy Carter/North Wind Picture Archives; p. 8 © Eric and David Hosking/CORBIS; pp. 11, 12, 16 Joslyn Art Museum, Omaha, Nebraska; p. 15 © CORBIS; p. 19 The Walters Art Museum, Baltimore, Maryland; p. 20 Hulton/Archive/Getty Images.

Maynard, Charles W. (Charles William), 1955–
Jim Bridger : frontiersman and mountain guide / Charles W. Maynard.—1st ed.
p. cm. — (Famous explorers of the American West)
  ISBN 0-8239-6288-1 (library binding)
1. Bridger, Jim, 1804–1881—Juvenile literature. 2. Pioneers—West (U.S.)—Biography—Juvenile literature. 3. Frontier and pioneer life—West (U.S.)—Juvenile literature. 4. Scouts and scouting—West (U.S.)—Biography—Juvenile literature. 5. Trappers—West (U.S.)—Biography—Juvenile literature. 6. West (U.S.)—Biography—Juvenile literature. [1. Bridger, Jim, 1804–1881. 2. Pioneers. 3. West (U.S.)—Biography. 4. West (U.S.)—Discovery and exploration.] I. Title. II. Series.
  F592.B85 M39 2003
  978'.02'092—dc21

Manufactured in the United States of America

CONTENTS

Young Bridger worked as a blacksmith in the 1820s. He learned to use ironworking tools, such as the ones a blacksmith holds in this photograph from the 1840s.

Bridger grew up in the wilderness near St. Louis, Missouri, which is pictured here in 1820.

EARLY LIFE

Jim Bridger was born on March 17, 1804, near Richmond, Virginia. His father owned a **tavern** and **surveyed** land. In 1812, when Jim was eight years old, his family moved west to Six-Mile Prairie, near St. Louis, Missouri. Six years later, Jim's mother became ill and died. Soon his father and brother died too, leaving Jim and his little sister as orphans. Their aunt took care of them. The frontier had no schools. Jim never learned to read or write.

As a teenager, Bridger worked on a river ferry as a **boatman**. He later **apprenticed** himself to a **blacksmith**. He learned to make horseshoes and other iron items. After working in a blacksmith's shop for four years, he moved to St. Louis, Missouri. In the 1820s, St. Louis was the Gateway to the West, and many people went there to start a new life.

LEARING THE FUR TRADE

In 1822, 18-year-old Jim Bridger heard about a newspaper **advertisement**. The ad called for "**Enterprising** Young Men" to go up the Missouri River to its source. Bridger did what the ad instructed and was hired to be a mountain man. Mountain men hunted and explored in the Rocky Mountains. They searched for beavers, whose pelts, or fur skins, were useful for making certain clothing.

Bridger learned to set beaver traps in the icy waters of mountain streams. In the summer of 1823, he was working with Andrew Henry's group of fur trappers. On the way to the Yellowstone River, a grizzly bear attacked Hugh Glass, a member of the group. Bridger and John Fitzgerald agreed to stay with Glass until he died. Frightened after seeing signs of warring Native Americans, they left Glass to die alone and returned to Henry's group. In the end Glass did not die but recovered enough to get back to safety.

Top: *Two mountain men have trapped a beaver.*

Left and Right: *Mountain men often wore clothing made from deerskin, called buckskin. Fringe sometimes decorated the sleeves and the pants.*

Norris Geyser Basin is in today's Yellowstone National Park. Among the wonders Bridger explored in this area in the 1830s were geysers, or underground springs that shoot hot water and steam into the air.

EXPLORING THE LAND

As Bridger hunted for beaver, he observed the mountains, the valleys, and the rivers of the West. His memory of the land helped him to find his way.

In 1824, he and other mountain men spent the winter with Native Americans who spoke of an easier way through the mountains. This led Bridger and others to South Pass. Robert Stuart first discovered this easy passage through the Rocky Mountains in 1812, but it had been forgotten.

In the winter of 1824, Bridger sailed down Bear River to the place where it emptied into a large lake. At first he believed the lake was the Pacific Ocean, because the water tasted salty. He later discovered it was the Great Salt Lake.

In the 1830s, he explored the Yellowstone Plateau's boiling springs. He also saw its **petrified** trees and huge waterfalls.

RENDEZVOUS

Beads, such as these from the trading post at Fort Mandan, South Dakota, were used often in trade with Native Americans.

Each summer from 1825 to 1840, the mountain men and some Native Americans gathered in a **rendezvous** for about two to three weeks. Traders brought goods such as traps, gunpowder, lead, and other supplies that the men needed. The trappers traded beaver pelts for the goods.

During the rendezvous, Native Americans camped with the mountain men. Many of the mountain men married Native American women. One year at a rendezvous, Jim Bridger married a Shoshone woman. They had several children.

The Crow people called Bridger Blanket Chief. Some believe he was called that because his coat was made from a blanket. Others think he got the name because he used blankets in trading with Native Americans at the rendezvous.

Often at the rendezvous the trappers competed in contests and traded furs. They also shared stories about their explorations and adventures.

Alfred Jacob Miller painted a group of mountain men meeting with Native Americans at a rendezvous in the 1830s. At these meetings, trappers and Native Americans traded furs for supplies.

Huge herds of bison and elk once roamed the upper region of the Missouri River. Their numbers shrank greatly as hunters killed these animals for their pelts.

NATIVE AMERICAN FRIENDS AND ENEMIES

Jim Bridger learned the customs and the languages of many Native American peoples. He tried to help his Native American friends by trading fairly with them and by respecting their land. Washakie, a Shoshone chief, and Bridger were friends. Washakie led the Shoshone in many battles and in working with the trappers and the settlers.

Some Native Americans fought the mountain men and the settlers. They felt the settlers were ruining their hunting areas and were killing all the **bison**. In an 1832 battle, Bridger was shot in the back with two arrows. His friends removed one arrowhead but could not get the other one out. Three years later on his way to Oregon, Dr. Marcus Whitman took out the iron arrowhead from Bridger's back.

13

FORT BRIDGER

By the 1840s, the fur trade began to die out. Fur clothing went out of style, and most of the fur-bearing animals in the West had been killed. Many people headed to Oregon and to California to set up farms or businesses. Mountain men, such as Bridger, guided them through the mountains and the deserts.

In 1843, Bridger joined Louis Vasquez, a trapper, in establishing a trading post on the Black Fork of the Green River. They built a **stockade** of 8-foot-high (2-m-high) logs with a few buildings inside the log walls.

When the **Mormons** came to Utah in 1847, Bridger told them how to get to the valley of the Great Salt Lake. The

Mormons took over the small post in 1853, after Bridger and Vasquez left the area. The stockade burned down in the Mormon War in 1857. General Albert S. Johnston built a military fort on the site of the old post. He named it Fort Bridger in honor of mountain man and guide Jim Bridger.

Fort Bridger served as a supply stop for travelers along the Oregon Trail in the mid-1800s. Bridger built a store inside the fort and stocked it with groceries, tobacco, bullets, and gunpowder.

In 1853, Jim Bridger's friend Louis Vasquez gave him a rifle as a gift. After Bridger's death, the rifle (above) was sold several times until it found a home in 1988, in the Museum of the Mountain Man in Pinedale, Wyoming.

Alfred Jacob Miller painted Jim Bridger, in a Suit of English Armor after seeing Bridger wear the armor at a rendezvous in 1837. Sir William Drummond Stewart had given Bridger the armor as a gift.

Bridger became famous for his knowledge of the West. His memory for places made him an excellent guide. He often drew maps of an area with charcoal on bison skins or with a stick in the sand. Even a Scottish nobleman, Sir William Drummond Stewart, asked Bridger to be his guide in 1832. Bridger took him to many places, including the area that later became Yellowstone National Park. Captain Howard Stansbury hired Bridger to guide his group through the Rockies in 1849. On this trip, in 1850, Bridger found a new pass in Wyoming that was easier to cross than South Pass. This pass was later named Bridger's Pass. It ran south from the Great Basin. It became part of the routes of the Overland Trail, the Pony Express, and the Union Pacific Railroad.

General Grenville Dodge described Jim Bridger as "a very companionable man. In person he was over six feet tall, spare, straight as an arrow, . . . eyes gray, hair brown and abundant even in old age, expression mild and manners agreeable. He was hospitable and generous, and was always trusted and respected."

As Jim Bridger grew older, almost everyone called him Old Gabe. Today nobody knows how or why Bridger got this **nickname**. Old Gabe often spoke about his adventures. He talked about the Yellowstone Plateau and described its bubbling mud, boiling springs, and mountain of glass, called **Obsidian** Cliff. Usually people did not believe him. They thought he was just telling a tall tale. Sometimes Bridger would make his memories into wild, silly stories.

Old Gabe Bridger often worked for the U.S. Army as a scout and an **interpreter**. The Army used his skills as an interpreter for the Treaty of Fort Laramie in 1851. His skills as an interpreter helped people who didn't speak the same language to understand one another.

General Grenville Dodge hired Bridger later to help plot the route of the Union Pacific Railroad. General Dodge and Bridger became good friends as Bridger guided Dodge through the Rockies.

Alfred Jacob Miller painted this inside view of the first Fort Laramie, built in 1834. Fort Laramie became an important trading and military post along the Oregon, California, and Mormon Trails.

TIMELINE

1804 On March 17, James Bridger is born in Richmond, Virginia.

1818 Jim Bridger's mother, father, and brother die.

1822 Bridger joins Ashley and Henry to become a fur trapper.

1824 Bridger crosses South Pass with mountain man Tom Fitzpatrick.

1833 Bridger traps on the Yellowstone Plateau, which later becomes Yellowstone National Park.

1843 Bridger and partner Louis Vasquez build Fort Bridger where the Overland Trail joins the Oregon Trail.

1851 Bridger acts as an interpreter for the U.S. government for the Treaty of Fort Laramie.

1859 Bridger begins guiding U.S. Army expeditions as a government scout.

1868 Bridger is discharged as a scout for the Army and returns to Missouri.

1881 On July 17, Jim Bridger dies on his farm near Kansas City, Missouri.

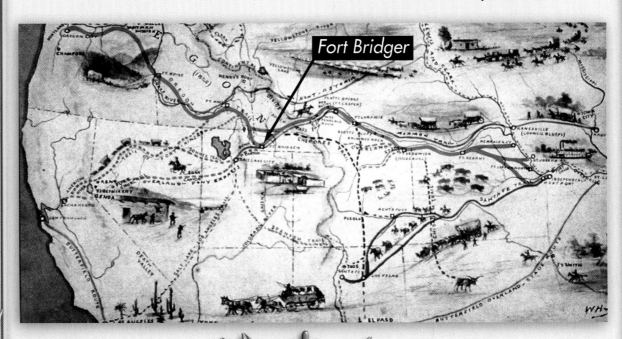

Fort Bridger

Jim Bridger established a small fort on the Green River in 1843. It became an important trading post and supply stop on the Oregon Trail.

FILLING IN THE MAP

Bridger had a brilliant mind and could remember landmarks and languages. He once hired someone to read him William Shakespeare's plays, and Bridger even learned by heart parts of these plays. He explored large sections of the West. During his long life, Bridger provided many valuable details to the existing maps of the United States.

In 1822, when Bridger began as a mountain man, most people in the United States knew little about the western parts of the nation. By the time Bridger bought a farm near Kansas City, Missouri, in 1868, many people could travel through the West because of Bridger's explorations. At that time the first railroad to cross the continent was almost complete. It followed a route Bridger had helped to scout.

By 1875, Bridger had completely lost his eyesight. He owned a dog that kept him from getting lost. Jim Bridger died on July 17, 1881. His old friend, General Dodge, built a monument at Bridger's grave so people would not forget him.

Bridger's name lives on in many places. These places include the Bridger Mountains, Bridger's Pass, and Bridger-Teton National Forest. Fort Bridger is now a Wyoming state historic site.

The railroad line and Interstate 80 still follow the route first **blazed** by Bridger. Many highways wind through mountain passes that he crossed long ago.

Jim Bridger was a mountain man, a guide, an interpreter, a storyteller, and a scout. He helped a young nation learn more about its new land and how to travel safely across it.

GLOSSARY

advertisement (ad-vur-TYZ-ment) A public notice that tells people about a product, an event, or something a person needs.

apprenticed (uh-PREN-tisd) Learned a skill from an older, more experienced person.

bison (BY-sun) A large, four-legged creature often called a buffalo, that has shaggy fur and is found on the Great Plains.

blacksmith (BLAK-smith) A person who makes and repairs iron objects with a hammer and an anvil.

blazed (BLAYZD) Made a mark on a tree or a rock to show a trail.

boatman (BOHT-mun) A person who worked on riverboats or ferries by pushing poles and pulling ropes to move the boat in the water.

enterprising (EN-tur-pryz-ing) Willing to do something for opportunity.

interpreter (in-TUR-pruh-ter) A person who explains the meaning of one language with another.

Mormons (MOR-munz) Members of a religious group founded in the United States by Joseph Smith in 1830.

nickname (NIK-naym) A funny and interesting name that is used instead of a person's real name.

obsidian (uhb-SIH-dee-un) A dark, glassy volcanic rock. The Obsidian Cliffs in Yellowstone National Park are made of this glassy rock.

petrified (PEH-trih-fyd) When something, such as wood, has turned to stone over thousands of years.

rendezvous (RON-day-voo) A French word that means an agreed place and time to meet.

stockade (stah-KAYD) A wooden wall made of large, strong posts that are put upright in the ground to protect the area inside the wall.

surveyed (ser-VAYD) To have measured land.

tavern (TA-vurn) A place to spend the night or to eat a meal.

23

INDEX

PRIMARY SOURCES

Page 4 (top). A photograph from the 1840s now in the Library of Congress in Washington, D.C., shows a blacksmith with his tools. **(bottom).** A hand-colored woodcut from 1820 shows Choteau's Point near St. Louis, Missouri. **Page 7 (bottom).** Frederic Remington drew these two mountain men after his years of travel in the West after 1880. **Page 11.** *The Cavalcade or Caravan.* Alfred Jacob Miller (1810–1874) painted this picture showing Sir William Drummond Stewart and a group of mountain men and Native Americans meeting in a supply caravan on the way to the spring 1837 rendezvous. Miller was the first artist to record the lives of the mountain men. Miller drew the scenes on the trail and later used them as the basis for oil paintings for Stewart's Murthly Castle in Scotland. **Page 12.** *Buffalo and Elk on the Upper Missouri.* Swiss artist Karl Bodmer painted this watercolor after his 1832–34 journey to the Missouri River. The picture is now at the Joslyn Art Museum in Omaha, Nebraska. **Page 16 (top).** Jim Bridger's rifle. This rifle is engraved with "J. Bridger 1853" and was given to Bridger as a gift by his partner, Louis Vasquez. Today it is in the collection of the Museum of the Mountain Man in Pinedale, Wyoming. **(bottom).** *Jim Bridger, in a Suit of English Armor.* Painted by Alfred Jacob Miller after he witnessed Bridger at the Rendezvous of 1837. **Page 19.** *Fort Laramie.* This interior view is the only one that exists of the first Fort Laramie and was painted by Alfred Jacob Miller in 1858–1860.

WEB SITES

To learn more about Jim Bridger, check out these Web sites:
http://xroads.virginia.edu/~HYPER/HNS/Mtmen/jimbrid.html
www.isu.edu/~trinmich/FtBridger.html